The Nature Kid's Guide to
ELEPHANTS

DAVID ANDERSON

LP Media Inc. Publishing
Text copyright © 2026 by LP Media Inc.

For information address LP Media Inc. Publishing,
30012 Variolite St NW, Princeton MN 55371
www.lpmedia.org

Publication Data

Elephants
The Nature Kid's Guide to Elephants — First edition.

Summary: "Learn all about Elephants, the Nature Kid Way"
— Provided by publisher.

ISBN: 979-8-89818-101-7

[1. Elephants – Non-Fiction] I. Title.

Title: The Nature Kid's Guide to Elephants

CONTENTS

SUNNY SAVANNAS

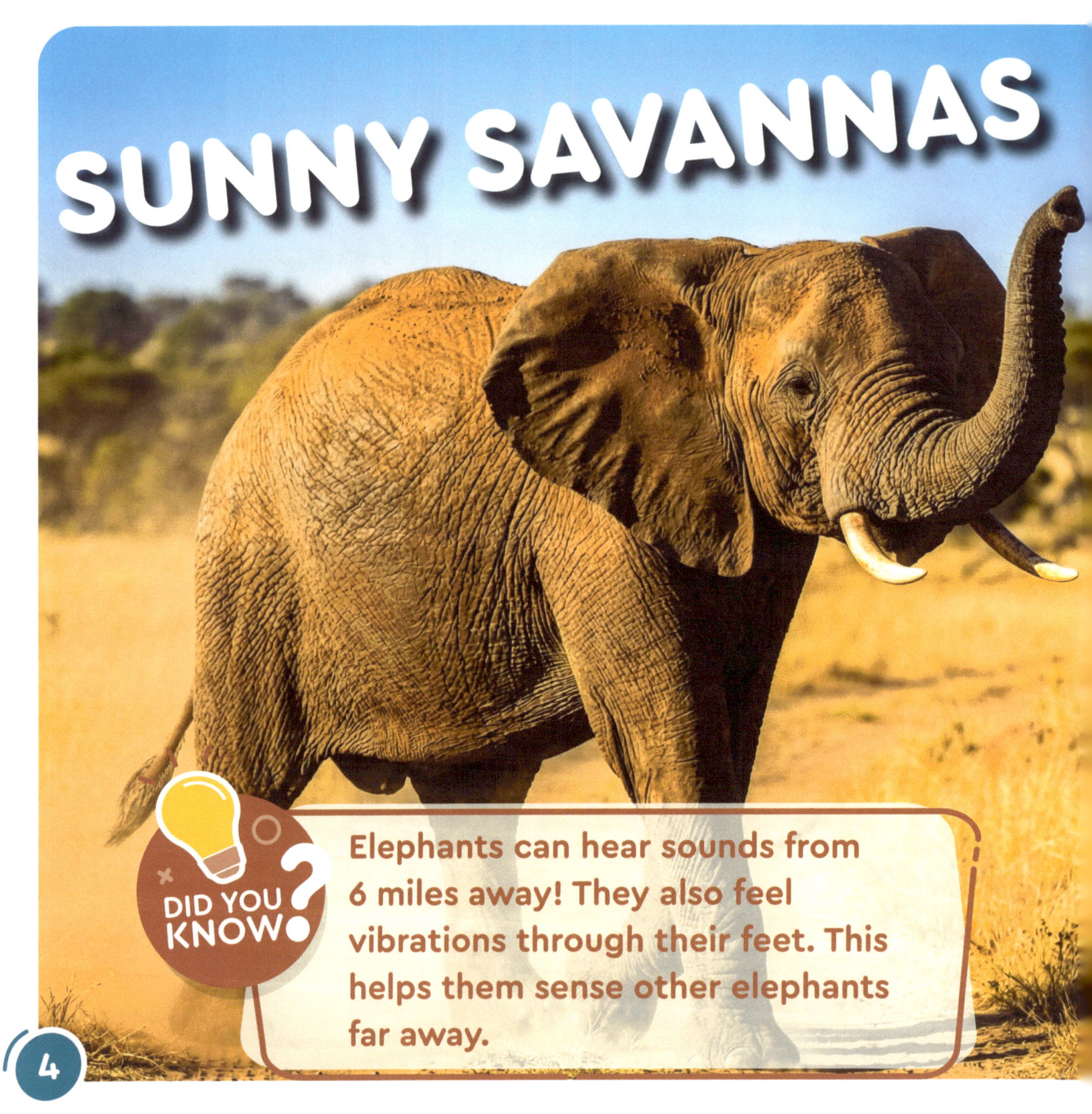

Stomp! A big elephant walks across the hot grassland.

Elephants can live in deserts, savannas, and jungles. African elephants roam savannas and forests. Asian elephants live in forests and grasslands too. Both types need lots of space to find food and water.

Savannas are flat lands with tall grass and trees that grow far apart. The sun shines bright and hot, so elephants rest in the shade during the hottest part of the day.

Water holes are important spots. Elephants drink and cool off there. They spray water on their backs and roll in mud. This helps protect their skin from the sun.

AFRICAN
ADVENTURES

Rumble! An elephant calls to its herd far away. The sound travels for miles.

African elephants live in about 37 countries in sub-Saharan Africa. They roam from Kenya to Botswana.

These elephant herds follow old paths that their families have used for many years. The paths connect feeding areas to rivers.

A herd may travel over 500 square miles in one year to find fresh plants and water.

The oldest female leads the herd. She remembers all the best paths to food and water!

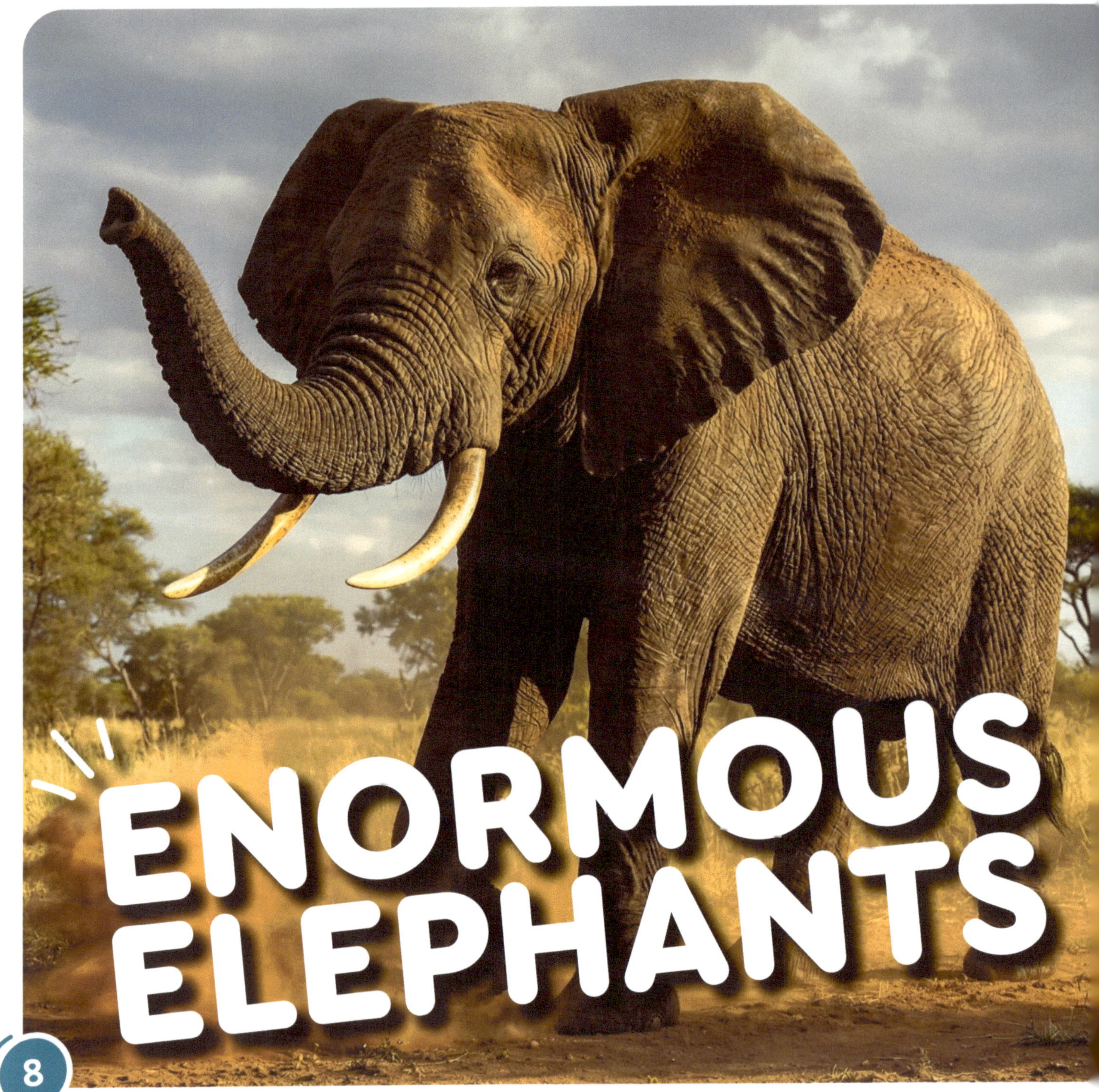

ENORMOUS
ELEPHANTS

Thump! A huge elephant shakes the ground with each step.

Elephants are the largest land animals on Earth. African elephants are bigger than Asian elephants. A male African elephant can weigh up to 12,000 pounds.

Elephants stand very tall. An adult African elephant can reach 13 feet high at the shoulder. That is taller than most ceilings.

Even baby elephants are big. A newborn calf weighs about 250 pounds. That is heavier than most grown ups!

An elephant's ear alone can be six feet long!

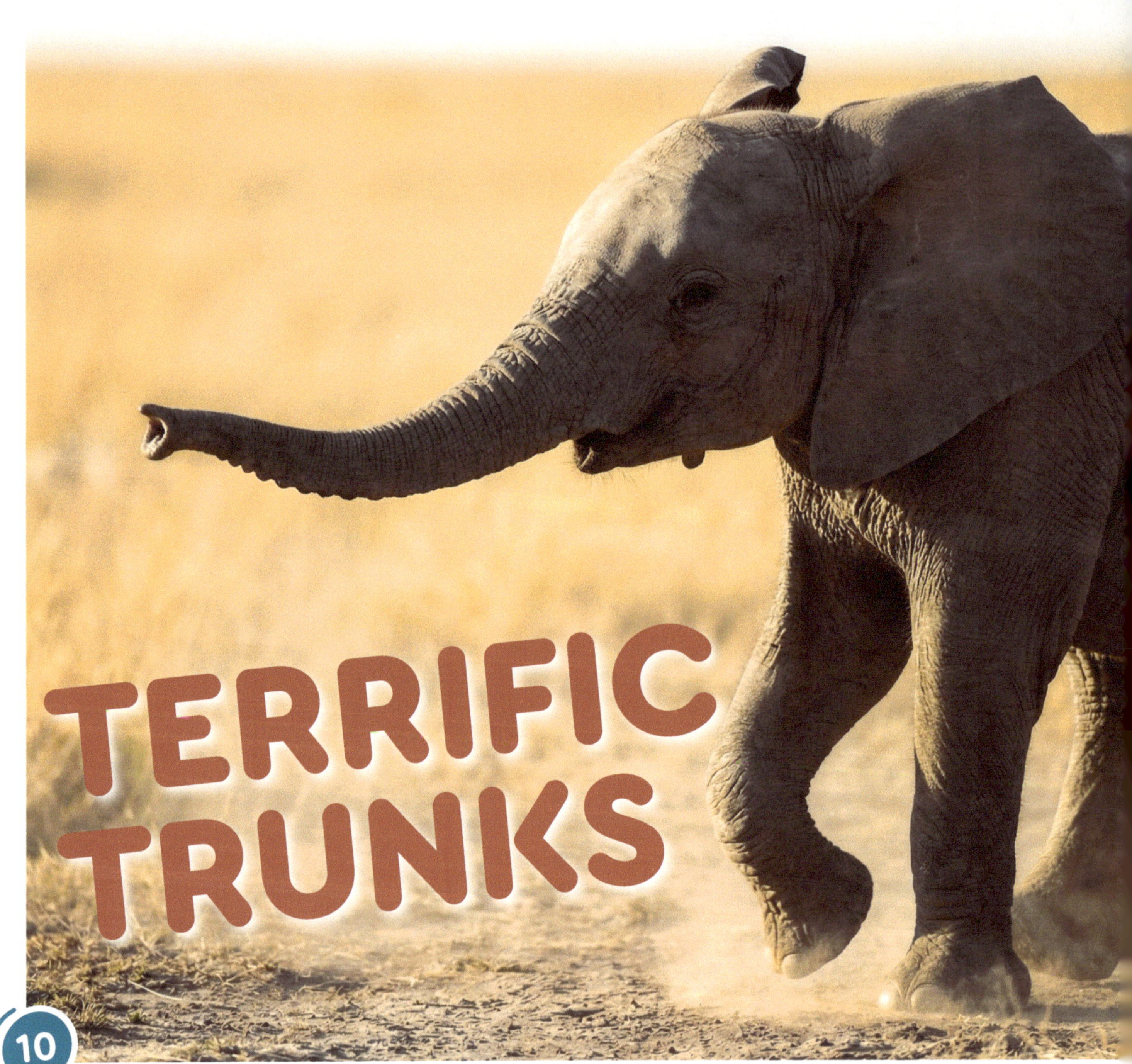

TERRIFIC
TRUNKS

Swoosh! A young elephant swings its long trunk through the air.

An elephant trunk has no bones inside. Instead, it has about 40,000 muscles. This makes the trunk very strong and flexible.

Elephants use their trunks in many ways. They breathe, smell, and make sounds with them. They also grab food and lift heavy things.

The trunk tip works like fingers. African elephants have two finger-like parts, while Asian elephants have one. These tips can pick up tiny seeds or single blades of grass.

Elephants can suck up two gallons of water in their trunks at once to drink!

SUPER
SNIFFERS

Sniff! An elephant lifts its trunk high into the air.

Elephants have an amazing sense of smell. They detect smells with their long trunks. They can even smell water from miles away!

Elephants smell the air to find food. They also sniff to detect danger nearby.

Elephants recognize family members by smell too. Each elephant has its own special scent.

Elephants can smell the difference between people who are dangerous and people who are friendly!

13

TOUGH
TUSKS

Crack! An elephant scrapes its tusk against a tree.

Elephants have two long tusks. These tusks are actually giant teeth. They grow throughout the elephant's whole life.

Tusks are made of **ivory**, which is very hard and strong. This makes them perfect for digging for water in dry ground.

Tusks also help elephants defend themselves. They can push away predators with their tusks. Male elephants sometimes clash tusks when they fight.

Elephant tusks can grow 10 feet long and weigh over 100 pounds each!

HUNGRY
HERBIVORES
16

Crunch! An elephant chews on a mouthful of leaves.

Elephants are **herbivores**. This means they only eat plants.

Elephants eat many kinds of plants. They munch on grasses, leaves, and bark. They also enjoy fruits and roots.

Elephants spend most of their day eating. They need lots of food because they are so big. An elephant can eat up to 330 pounds of food daily!

Elephants dig wells with their feet for water!

STOMP AND TALK
18

Thump! An elephant stomps its big foot on the ground.

Elephants make many sounds. They trumpet loudly when excited or scared. They also rumble in low, deep tones. These rumbles travel far across the land.

Some elephant sounds are too low for humans to hear. Other elephants can hear these sounds from miles away. This helps herds stay in touch.

Elephants also talk with their bodies. They flap their ears when angry. They touch trunks to say hello. A raised trunk can mean danger is near.

Stomping sends messages through the ground. Other elephants feel these vibrations with their feet.

WATCH OUT

DID YOU KNOW?
Elephants will throw sticks and rocks with their trunks to scare predators!

20

Growl! A lion watches an elephant herd from far away.

Adult elephants have few predators. This is because they are too big for most animals to attack. Baby elephants need to watch out though.

Lions sometimes hunt young elephants. Crocodiles may grab calves near water. Hyenas also watch for weak or small elephants.

Adult elephants protect the herd. They stand together and face danger. Their size scares most predators away.

Healthy adult elephants are very safe because their large bodies keep them protected.

CIRCLE UP

Trumpet! An elephant raises its trunk and calls out loud.

Elephants have a special way to stay safe. When danger comes, they form a circle.

Adult elephants stand on the outside. They face outward toward the threat. The baby elephants stay safe in the middle.

This circle protects the young calves. The adults use their big bodies as shields. Herds work together to keep everyone safe.

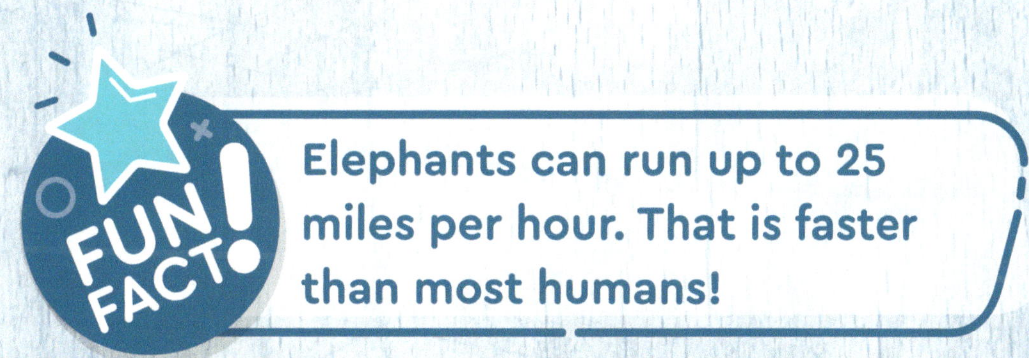

24

Splash! An elephant steps into a muddy river. The water feels cool.

Elephant legs are like strong pillars. Each foot has soft padding underneath. The pads are like elephant shoes!

The padding helps elephants walk quietly. It also cushions their heavy bodies.

Elephants usually walk slowly, but they can also run when needed. When looking for food or water, elephants travel up to 30 miles each day.

Elephants can swim! They use their trunks like snorkels to breathe above the water.

DAY BY DAY

Snort! An elephant dusts its back with dirt. The dust keeps bugs away.

Elephants have busy days. They spend most of their time eating and walking.

Elephants eat for 12 to 18 hours daily. They need lots of food because they are so big. Finding enough plants takes a long time.

Elephants also rest during the hottest part of the day. They stand in the shade or near water. At night, elephants sleep for only a few hours.

Elephants take mud baths to cool down and protect their skin. The mud blocks the sun and keeps bugs away.

HERD HEROES

Grunt! A group of elephants walks together in a line.

Elephants live in groups called herds. A herd is like a big family.

The oldest female leads the herd. She is called the **matriarch**. She remembers where to find food and water.

Herds can have 8 to 100 elephants. Sisters, daughters, and aunts stay together.

Males leave the herd once they grow up.

Baby elephants stay with their mothers for about 16 years. One of the longest bonds in the animal kingdom!

FINDING LOVE
30

Whoosh! A male elephant flaps his ears wide. He is looking for a mate.

Male elephants leave their herds as teenagers. They live alone or with other males until they are ready to mate.

Males may not successfully mate until they are around 20 to 25 years old. They find females by following their smell and sound.

Female elephants can have babies every 4 to 5 years. Babies can be born anytime of the year, not just in the spring like many animals.

Male elephants go through a time called musth. During musth, they are ready to mate.

CUTE
CALVES

Squeak! A baby elephant stays close to its mother.

Baby elephants are called calves. They are born after almost two years inside their mothers. That is the longest of any land animal.

Newborn calves weigh about 250 pounds. Even at this size, they can stand within one hour of being born. Calves drink their mother's milk for the first two years.

As they grow, calves learn by watching older elephants. They copy how adults eat, drink, and use their trunks.

DID YOU KNOW? A newborn elephant calf is about 3 feet tall. It grows quickly and gains 2 to 3 pounds every day.

MIGHTY MOMS

Rustle! A mother elephant gently nudges her calf with her trunk.

Mother elephants are very caring. They protect their calves from danger. They also teach them important skills like finding water.

Mothers nurse their young for about two years. But calves stay close to their mothers for much longer. Some daughters never leave.

Other females in the herd help raise **calves** too. Aunts and older sisters watch over young ones. This teamwork helps keep all the babies safe and healthy.

Mother elephants are pregnant longer than any other land mammal.

LOSING LAND

Snap! A fence blocks an elephant's path. It cannot reach the trees.

Elephants need large spaces to live. They travel many miles each day to find food and water.

People build farms where elephants once roamed. Fences now cut across elephant paths. This makes it hard for herds to move.

When elephants lose their land, they may enter villages. This causes problems for both elephants and people.

Elephants need up to 1,000 square miles to roam. Some herds in Africa travel across five different countries!

HELPING HERDS

Click! A ranger takes a photo of an elephant herd.

People around the world help elephants. Scientists study herds to learn what they need. Rangers guard elephants from harm.

Some groups create safe paths for elephants. These **corridors** connect wild areas, so elephants can travel more freely.

Many countries have made new laws to protect elephants and their homes. With help, elephant numbers can grow.

FUN FACT!

Some protected areas show about 20 percent elephant population growth over ten years.

GLOSSARY

savannas
Flat lands with tall grass and trees that grow far apart.

herbivores
Animals that only eat plants.

matriarch
The oldest female elephant who leads the herd.

corridors
Safe paths that connect wild areas so animals can travel between them.

calves
Baby elephants.

ivory
The hard, white material that elephant tusks are made of.

musth
A time when male elephants have extra hormones that make them ready to mate